A
Prep

"This is exactly the type of communication guide the new parents I work with need! Becoming a family is difficult, and the couple's relationship often suffers. When using this book, much of the relationship stress could be alleviated in the postpartum period, and the whole family would be happier. I think this book should be **required reading** for all new parents."

~ Dr. Jay Warren, creator of *Connecting with Baby During Pregnancy* online course, *Pregnancy, Birth and Infancy from the Baby's Perspective* online course, *Healthy Births, Healthy Babies* podcast, and *The Dadhood Journey* podcast

"If there is one book expectant parents should have on their shelf to learn how to move from a pregnant couple to a parenting family, it's this one. This resource is so accessible, easy to navigate, and all-inclusive. Parenting can be a challenge in today's world, and these conversations are essential for the health and well-being of the whole family. We both just wish we'd had this resource available when we were first expecting!"

~ Jayme Crockett, Birth Photographer, Mother of 8, and Student Midwife, *and*
~ Holly Lammer, RN, PPNE, Childbirth Educator, and Yoga Teacher
~ co-hosts of the *Mindful Birth Peaceful Earth* podcast

"An honest, down-to-earth manual for anyone thinking of having a child. Reading this book is like talking with a good friend or therapist who knows the territory because she has lived it and thought deeply about it. I am really happy that a book like this is finally available."

~ Thomas R. Verny, MD, DHL (Hon), DPsych,
fellow of the Royal College of Physicians of Canada,
fellow of the American Psychiatric Association,
co-founder and president emeritus of the Association of
Prenatal and Perinatal Psychology and Health,
author of international bestseller,
The Secret Life of the Unborn Child with John Kelly,
Parenting Your Unborn Child,
and two books with Pamela Weintraub:
Nurturing Your Unborn Child and *Pre-Parenting:
Nurturing Your Child from Conception*

"This is a significant and profound book that has the potential to transform parenting from conflict and struggle to harmony and health. But even more so, it epitomizes and illuminates that children become what they live. I recommend this book to all prospective and current parents."

~ Dr. William R. Emerson, Clinical Psychologist,
co-founder and president emeritus of the Association of
Prenatal and Perinatal Psychology and Health,
National Science Foundation winner for
Contributions to Psychology, and pioneer in
prenatal and perinatal psychology

"This thoughtful book is an invaluable resource for expectant parents and will help build a strong foundation for babies and their families."

~ Dr. Annie Brook, author of *Birth's Hidden Legacy*,
somatic psychologist, play and family therapist, and
founder of *The Somatic Attachment Training*

"Not only is this book a key for rewarding parenting, but I believe it would be a great start for anyone leaning toward a long-term relationship."

~ Barbara C. Decker, HypnoBirthing Childbirth Educator,
Pre- and Perinatal Educator, and
Certified Prenatal Bonding (BA) Facilitator

"This is a book that could support a couple for years as they navigate discussions about evolving values, changing circumstances, and the multitude of roles becoming parents brings into their lives. *Preparing for Parenthood* will support couples in spending more time enjoying their family lives and less time having unexpected arguments. It is a wonderful resource for getting parents to connect around all things related to parenting before problems arise."

~ Ellen Boeder, MA, LPC,
PACT Level 3 couple's therapist, and
faculty at The Relationship School

Preparing for Parenthood

Preparing for Parenthood

55 Essential Conversations
for
Couples Becoming Families

by
Stephanie Dueger, PhD

Printed in the United States of America.

Published by Author Academy Elite
PO Box 43, Powell, OH 43035
www.AuthorAcademyElite.com

Identifiers:
LCCN: 2020910019
ISBN: 978-1-64746-318-2 (paperback)
ISBN: 978-1-64746-319-9 (hardback)
ISBN: 978-1-64746-320-5 (ebook)

Available in paperback, hardcover, e-book, and audiobook.

Interior design by Jetlaunch.
Cover design by Twaalf" at 99Designs.

To Dan, for co-creating a beautiful foundation of
marriage and parenthood with me,

and to Kaitlyn and Braelyn,
for making the amazing journey of parenting
my most treasured.

Supplemental materials,

such as worksheets, videos, and other extras

related to this book, as well as more information

about Dr. Dueger's work, can be found on her

website, at

www.drduegertherapy.com

Contents

Acknowledgments

My sincere appreciation goes to Ellen Boeder, Jill Dawson, Suzanne Forrester, Marnie Huffman-Greene, Caitlin Kline, Dan Riggan, Jenni Skyler, Ciara Wentworth, and Robyn Wilkinson for allowing me to interview them about what would have made the transition to parenthood easier. Thank you also to the many clients in sessions and friends on hikes who were willing to share their experiences and challenges of parenting with me.

I want to express my gratitude to my helpful and honest beta readers, Jill Dawson, Erica Dueger, Marnie Huffman-Greene, and Dan Riggan, who highlighted where I could hone my writing and add substance. A special thanks goes to Shari Caudron for her coaching and editing support throughout this process, and to Felicity Fox for line and copy editing.

Thank you to my family of origin—Erica, Caroline, and Walter Dueger—for their extensive feedback, ongoing support, and love. And my deepest love and appreciation go to my immediate family—Dan, Kaitlyn, and Braelyn—who are the sustenance of my entire world and who never stopped encouraging me to birth this "third baby."

My husband and I became parents for the first time in the summer of 2007. We were at once thrilled, grateful, and *completely* overwhelmed. Although we were mature, well-prepared, and extremely excited to be parents, we were both humbled at how challenging this transition to parenthood was for us. Like many first-time parents, we learned that weaving the constant needs of a newborn infant into a family that previously included only two busy adults would stretch us in ways we'd never imagined. We quickly realized parenthood was a journey we would need to experience and adjust to on a day-to-day basis.

Welcoming an infant into what had been a stable and relatively easy system to negotiate required massive family reorganization. It took many months to become comfortable adjusting to the myriad practical and emotional needs of this new family system. Ultimately, we discovered many of our adult needs, such as daily exercise or ample sleep, would have to be placed on the back burner for a while to properly care for our small daughter with the love and attention she deserved and needed.

While we expected changes to occur, the actual *lived* experience was a bit more shocking. The first six weeks or so postpartum, I was awake much of every night learning to nurse our baby, discovering what her different cries meant, and healing from the birth. Days seemed to disappear quickly, one after the other. Two-to-six months postpartum, my husband and I tried to remember what it felt like to sleep through the night. Many of our daily conversations changed from nurturing our connection to managing the business of parenthood. While we were honored and elated to be parents, and bonding with our daughter was a blissful experience, we were also spending a lot of time struggling.

As a prolific reader and researcher, I devoured nearly every book available about pregnancy, birth, and early parenthood before having our first child. With an extensive background in education, psychology, and pre- and perinatal health, I never had fewer than ten library books on my bedside table. And because my husband and I are both trained psychotherapists, we were skilled at having in-depth discussions about all of life's nuances.

However, there were many conversations about parenthood I wished we'd had *before* our first daughter arrived, rather than trying to hash through them when we were both sleep-deprived and stretched to our limits after our baby was born. For example, we both had unspoken expectations about the different roles we played in our relationship prior to our daughter's birth, such as whose turn it was to cook, pay bills, or pick up the groceries. Because of these expectations, we'd neglected to talk about what would happen when everything changed once our baby arrived. Now who was going to handle the enormous mountain of laundry that appeared on a daily basis? Who was going to walk the dog (who was already moping around, letting us know she felt her status as our first baby had been unfairly usurped)? Before having a baby, we had always managed to fit in activities, such as seeing friends or going for a long hike. Yet we had not discussed how our free time might drastically shift after our daughter arrived, and, perhaps more importantly, how we could best support each other to get our needs met in this new phase of our relationship. In short, we didn't know what we didn't know.

Since that time, many years ago, we've realized we were not alone. Nearly every parent I have spoken with, whether friend or client, has shared similar stories about the challenging transition to parent-hood, and how unprepared they felt for the massive lifestyle changes. We certainly had many periods of new-parent bliss. But the overwhelming uncertainty we also experienced after our first daughter was born took us by surprise. Then, I realized something. In all of my reading and researching, I found very little information designed to help couples discover their way as parents by consciously thinking and talking about their hopes and expectations for their family prior to bringing a little human into the world. No wonder I, and so many of my friends and clients, felt overwhelmed. Parenthood is too huge a rite of passage to jump in without feeling as prepared as possible.

The intention of this book is to fill this preparation gap by helping facilitate discussions between couples in a supportive, non-judgmental, and easily-digestible way. Rather than imposing a particular philosophy of parenting, I hope to provide you and your partner with conversation-starters to help you find your own way of becoming the parents you wish to be. While I hold opinions, I strongly believe people need to make decisions about what works best for them and their families. This book offers an invitation to dive deeply into conversations with your partner so you can begin to approach the parenting journey from the same perspective. Though my husband and I had some of the conversations included in this book, I wish we'd had many more of them *before* becoming parents. I learned about the importance of these conversations by asking other couples what they wished they had talked about prior to becoming parents.

The book is divided into seventeen focused sections, beginning with the couple relationship, moving through the preparation for parenthood, and finishing with the early postpartum experience. Each section includes several conversation-starters and an explanation about why the particular topic of conversation is important. Each conversation-starter then offers a practical action item to help you address the topic. The intention of this book is to prompt open discussions between you and your partner about topics you may or may not have thought through and shared with each other already. It will also provide ideas about how to address those topics on a practical level together.

Some of the topics discussed in this book would be beneficial for most couples at any point in their relationship. However, having these conversations before welcoming your first child can help relieve some of the additional stress that may arise. When you know you and your partner are on the same page, and you have clarity around your parenting styles and plans as a family, you can focus more of your energy on the critical tasks of being present for your child and taking care of yourself.

Some of the conversation-starters may stir up complicated feelings about such things as your family of origin, past trauma, or differences in your values and beliefs. Working through this book with your partner may also, at times, bring up conflict. If you find yourself emotionally upset about something from the past, or you and your partner feel stuck on a topic and unable to move through conflict, I encourage you to find outside emotional support. A trusted friend or therapist can help you to navigate these feelings.

Whether you choose to complete the book in order from cover-to-cover or select the topics of most interest and relevance to you and your partner, this book can help you yield tremendous benefits in approaching parenting as a unified team. As parents, you will both have a profound impact on your child and be forever changed by them. Yes, the parenting journey can have challenges. But with thorough preparation, your experience as a new parent can also be filled with greater ease, confidence, and a more powerful, loving connection with your partner.

In an attempt to be most inclusive of all family constellations, as well as for the ease of the reader, I have chosen to use the gender-neutral pronoun "they" in place of the pronouns "he" or "she" in the conversations and action items throughout the book. I have used the phrase "birth mother" throughout the book to address the individual carrying the baby during pregnancy. When speaking of my own and my family's experience, I use the pronouns we have accepted for ourselves.

The Couple
Relationship

Communication

The premise of this book is that having important conversations with each other about becoming parents will help you both fortify the foundation of your relationship and plan for your family's dreams and goals. Being engaged in a healthy relationship with an intimate partner is usually one of the most vital and desirable aspects of life. Solid communication is one of the two pillars that create a strong relationship foundation. (The other pillar is intimacy, which we'll discuss next.)

Communication is the area that tends to require the most attention in a relationship, and when neglected, can cause some of the greatest challenges between couples. When couples fail to honestly and regularly discuss their needs, feelings, and experiences with one another, anger, resentment, and distance can arise between them. Over time, relationships with poor communication often become tense and conflicted, or they break down altogether.

Understanding your own and your partner's communication style, your strengths as individuals and as a couple, and areas you would benefit from communication practice can be immensely helpful. My hope is that you will be able to build your communication skills, so you feel a greater connection to each other as you navigate the challenges that will undoubtedly arise in your lives together as parents. With improved communication in your relationship, you will be able to more confidently and competently approach the difficult topics that follow.

I have divided this section into six conversation topics: daily communication, communication during stress or conflict, emotional regulation, resolving and repairing conflicts, asking for needs to be met, and modeling good communication for your child. Many parents find some of these areas of communication challenging during their child's first three years, which is why I encourage you to spend some quality time on these topics with your partner *before* your baby arrives.

The Background: Communication 101: Learning to Share and Listen Well

Healthy communication involves taking responsibility for your feelings, avoiding blame, listening to your partner without interruption, and reflecting what you heard them say until they feel heard and understood. If there is conflict, healthy communication also involves requesting what you need in the future, as well as repairing any damage the conflict may have caused. Repair is a process that includes a specific and heartfelt apology, followed by statements about what you both agree to do differently next time.

It is helpful to be aware of your tone of voice and body language while you are communicating. Try to be gentle, respectful, and open with your tone, while also being clear and direct with your message. Body language that shows you want connection and repair, even if you are angry, is supportive of good communication as well. (Consider the difference in communication when someone avoids eye contact, has their arms crossed, and snaps at their partner, versus someone who maintains eye contact, has a more relaxed body position, and speaks in a gentle and direct way.) This can take practice. Many psychotherapists, myself included, often teach clients this process in session.

As you move through the conversations that follow in the book, you can use this process if a conflict arises in the discussion. I invite you to examine and try this method, even if it feels a bit cumbersome at first. Practice using this process several times with minor issues until you are feeling confident and skilled in resolving conflict.

Begin by choosing a topic together. Then, measure the level of charge around this conflict for each of you. For example, if taking out the garbage tends to cause an argument, have each partner choose a number between one and ten, relative to how upset the usual conflict around this topic makes them feel. Settle on practicing with a topic that has a low charge for both partners. Then, test the process with more charged topics to see if you are still able to resolve the conflict well.

If the conflict becomes too heated, take a break and decide on a time to get back together to continue the discussion. As you continue to practice this skill, you may find you are better able to manage your escalated emotions and work through very challenging conversations more easily.

Try to consistently focus on kindness and connection with your partner during conflict resolution. The intent is to build bridges between the two of you, not burn them down. I invite you to practice using this process when you have a challenging issue because it can help slow down the conflict and hear each other, which allows both partners to feel respected. Conflict can feel messy, but it can also lead to growth and greater connection.

The Process: Communication 101: Learning to Share and Listen Well

Partner 1: (The partner who feels a strong reaction to something their partner has said or done). Take responsibility for your experience and feelings. Explain how this interaction or event affected you. Avoid blaming.

"I felt _____ when you (said or did) _____."

(Rather than: "You always do _____!")

Partner 2: Avoid interrupting your partner while they speak. When they have finished speaking, say back to your partner what you heard them say to you, but in your own words. Try to address the underlying feelings your partner is conveying.

> "I heard you say _____. Is that cor-
> rect?" Avoid defending yourself. "It sounds
> as if that made you feel angry." Or, "I hear
> you feel really sad about that."
> (Rather than: "Well I wouldn't have
> _____ if you didn't _____." Or,
> "It's no big deal. You shouldn't be angry.")

Partner 1: Let your partner know whether they heard you correctly. Clarify, if necessary.

Partner 2: Let your partner know how you feel after hearing this, and share your experience.

> "I feel _____ to hear that. My experi-
> ence was _____."

Partner 1: Avoid interrupting your partner while they speak. Say back to your partner what you heard them say to you, but in your words.

> "I heard you say _____. Is that correct?"

<u>Partner 2</u>: Let your partner know whether they heard you correctly. Clarify, if necessary.

<u>Partner 1</u>: Let your partner know how you feel after hearing this information.

Continue this process until both of you feel fully heard by each other. Now, take turns requesting what you need in the future. Negotiate with each other to find what is workable for both of you.

"In the future, I would prefer/appreciate if you _____ ."

Then repair. A repair looks like a specific apology, followed by what you can do differently. Again, be aware of your tone and body language, which may convey more than your actual words do.

For example: "I'm sorry you felt hurt when I said that. I'll try to be more sensitive when we talk about _____ ."

Communication
Conversations

Conversation 1

How do you and your partner communicate on a daily basis? For example, how do you greet and say goodbye to each other? Do you easily share all of the details about your days? Does one of you tend to share more than the other? What is the emotional tone of your average daily conversation: upbeat, excited, stressed, tired, relaxed, irritable, etc.?

Action Item

Using the next two pages (one page for each of you), write down your experience of the way you communicate on a daily basis with your partner. Then, write down your experience of how your partner communicates with you. Are there changes you would like to see in the way you communicate with your partner or the way they communicate with you? Write these down in a non-judgmental way, where you take responsibility for your own experience. "I feel _____." (Use the Communication 101 process as a guide.) Then, share these with your partner.

Communication

Conversation 2

How do you communicate with your partner when under stress or during a conflict? Do you tend to quarrel, avoid one another, get snippy, or a combination? Do you tend to argue about the same thing(s) again and again? Do you avoid talking about certain topics for fear of arguing, or perhaps because you've felt shut down by your partner in the past?

Action Item

Using the next two pages (one page for each of you), write down how you communicate with your partner under stress or during a conflict. Then write down your experience of how your partner communicates with you when under stress or in conflict. What are the things you tend to argue about frequently? Are there changes you would like to see in the way you communicate with your partner during these times or the way they communicate with you? Write these down in a non-judgmental way, where you take responsibility for your own experience. "I feel _____." (Use the Communication 101 process as a guide.) Then, share these with your partner.

Communication

Conversation 3

How do you try to manage your emotions or regulate yourself during conflict, and how successful are you? For example, do you take deep breaths, tell your partner you need some time to calm down, and agree to come back at a certain time? Do you shut down during conflict, or have trouble regulating yourself, perhaps becoming very outwardly angry?

Action Item

Using the next two pages (one page for each of you),
write down how you try to manage your emotions or
regulate yourself during conflict and how successful
you believe you are with this. Are there changes you
would like to see in yourself during these times? Share
these with your partner. Then, let your partner know
if there are ways you could use support.

Communication

Conversation 4

How do you tend to resolve or repair conflicts with each other? Does one of you tend to reach out to the other partner more often to initiate an apology and reconnect after an argument? Are you both able to accept an attempt at repair (a specific apology, followed by what you can agree to do differently in the future), even if it's not perfect? Does the process of repairing feel satisfactory to both of you?

Action Item

Using the next two pages (one page for each of you), write down both how you currently experience repair, and how you prefer to experience repair in your relationship. Share this with your partner, and request changes if the repairing process doesn't feel satisfactory. (Use the Communication 101 process as a guide.)

Communication

Conversation 5

How successful are you at asking for your needs to be met or asking for support? Is this something that comes easily and naturally to you?

Action Item

If it is difficult for you to ask for support for your needs to be met, practice. Let your partner know that at least once per day you will ask them for help or support, even if you know you could do a particular task by yourself. For example, ask for help with such tasks as making dinner or folding clothes, or ask for emotional support, such as a hug. See if you can build your tolerance for both asking for help and gracefully accepting the support offered.

Conversation 6

In what ways do you imagine you would like to improve your communication as a couple as you become parents? Consider the way your communication with each other affects you. How do you imagine it will affect your child? What kind of communication skills would you like to model for your child?

Action Item

Using the next two pages (one page for each of you), write down the communication skills you would like to model for your child and support them in developing. Share these with your partner and discuss how you can begin to develop skills you may be lacking.

Communication

Intimacy

If communication is one of the two critical pillars of your relationship foundation, intimacy is the other. While there are varying definitions and interpretations of intimacy, in this context, intimacy refers to a deep level of closeness and connection to your partner. Without this sense of closeness and connection, your relationship would likely feel very lonely, and the foundation would feel unstable. Intimacy rewards the pleasure-center in your brain. It is what keeps you coming back for more, and what helps carry you through difficult disturbances in your primary relationship.

Intimacy is not only about sex. Intimacy can involve many kinds of desired physical touch, such as hugging, holding hands, or massage. It can also include the tenderness that may arise by maintaining gentle eye contact, having a quiet dinner or walk together, or feeling connected after a good laugh. These two critical pillars of your relationship foundation—communication and intimacy—support and sustain each other, and both benefit from focused attention. Solid communication and intimate connection, when combined, allow you to feel deeply attached and fulfilled in your partnership.

Basic Intimacy Exercise

I invite you to sit with your partner when you have a little uninterrupted time together. Face your partner, and take a few breaths, settling your nervous system. Invite your partner to do the same. Begin by making some gentle eye contact with each other, and if it feels comfortable, make some physical contact—hold hands, or place your hands on each other's knees. Share something with your partner you appreciate about them. Try to open your hearts to each other, so you and your partner can feel each other's presence when you are sharing. If any part of this feels uncomfortable, try sitting next to each other and making some gentle physical contact, such as one person resting their head on the other's shoulder.

Intimacy Conversations

Conversation 7

What is your current experience of intimacy with your partner? Do you talk openly with one another about your needs for intimacy of all kinds (sex, cuddling, shoulder rubs, feeling emotionally connected), and do you feel like your partner tries to meet these needs? How often do you have sex, and is the intimacy mutually satisfying for you as a couple? How often do you hold hands, give each other non-sexual touch, and make sustained eye contact with one another? What is the quality of your intimacy? Do you feel connected to each other?

Action Item

Complete the following grids. Discuss your answers together.

Partner A
Number of times per week/month we have sexual intimacy:
Number of times per week/month I would like to have sexual intimacy:
How I feel about our connection during sexual intimacy: 0 = not connected at all   3 = connected   5 = deeply connected
How I would like to feel about our connection during sexual intimacy:
Number of times per week/month we have non-sexual affection:
hugging:
cuddling:
holding hands:
other:
Number of times per week/month I would like to have non-sexual affection:
hugging:
cuddling:
holding hands:
other:
How I feel about our connection during non-sexual intimacy: 0 = not connected at all   3 = connected   5 = deeply connected
How I would like to feel about our connection during non-sexual intimacy:

Partner B
Number of times per week/month we have sexual intimacy:
Number of times per week/month I would like to have sexual intimacy:
How I feel about our connection during sexual intimacy: 0 = not connected at all   3 = connected   5 = deeply connected
How I would like to feel about our connection during sexual intimacy:
Number of times per week/month we have non-sexual affection:
hugging:
cuddling:
holding hands:
other:
Number of times per week/month I would like to have non-sexual affection:
hugging:
cuddling:
holding hands:
other:
How I feel about our connection during non-sexual intimacy: 0 = not connected at all   3 = connected   5 = deeply connected
How I would like to feel about our connection during non-sexual intimacy:

Conversation 8

Often, couples' sex lives change during pregnancy. Due to hormonal fluctuations, some pregnant mothers and partners experience an increased sex drive, and some experience a decreased sex drive. Feeling nauseous or uncomfortable during some stages of pregnancy is not uncommon. At times, even couples who have been assured they are having a healthy, normal pregnancy might have reservations about having sex or having certain kinds of sex during pregnancy. Discuss how you imagine your sex life, and intimacy in general, might change during the three trimesters of pregnancy. Discuss how you might address changes or concerns that arise during these times.

Action Item

Create a tentative, flexible plan for how you might try to stay intimately connected if events arise during pregnancy that impact your ability to share what was once your usual sex life.

Conversation 9

A birth mother's body will look and feel different, at least for a while, after having a baby. The birth mother may experience tenderness or pain, a lack of sleep, and needing time to heal from the birth experience. A desire for intimacy may be reduced as well, with more energy often needed for the baby. A partner may also feel many shifts. Usually, health care professionals advise waiting at least four to six weeks after birth to resume sex, depending upon the birth mother's healing process. How might you expect your sex life, and intimacy in general, will change after your baby is born?

Action Item

Create a tentative, flexible plan for how you might try to stay intimately connected if events arise in the postpartum period causing you to make changes in your sex life.

Conversation 10

Sometimes, residual pain or other complications may occur after the traditional four- to six-week healing time postpartum for resuming sex. What is your plan for navigating this challenge if it occurs?

Action Item

Complete the following grids. Discuss your answers together.

Birth Mother: If residual pain or complications occur for me following the four- to six-week healing time:
I am good at asking for my needs around intimacy to be met and would feel comfortable asking my partner for what I need.
I am not very good at asking for my needs to be met. I would hope my partner would realize on their own what my needs are and try to meet those needs.
I am good at setting boundaries related to my body and intimacy. I would feel comfortable telling my partner I am not ready for sexual intimacy.
I am not very good at setting boundaries related to my body and intimacy. I would hope my partner would realize on their own what I want or don't want and respect that.

If you answered that you are not very good at asking for your needs to be met, or at setting boundaries for yourself, come up with a plan with your partner around how you can support each other in respecting and meeting each other's needs.

Partner: If residual pain or complications occur for my partner following the four- to six-week healing time:
I am good at asking for my needs around intimacy to be met and would feel comfortable asking my partner for what I need.
I am not very good at asking for my needs to be met. I would hope my partner would realize on their own what my needs are and try to meet those needs.
I am good at setting boundaries related to my body and intimacy. I would feel comfortable telling my partner I am not ready for sexual intimacy.
I am not very good at setting boundaries related to my body and intimacy. I would hope my partner would realize on their own what I want or don't want and respect that.

If you answered that you are not very good at asking for your needs to be met, or at setting boundaries for yourself, come up with a plan with your partner around how you can support each other in respecting and meeting each other's needs.

Finances

Finances can be a sensitive topic that can cause significant stress and discourse in a relationship. In fact, finances are one of the most common reasons why couples argue. Many factors can impact a couple's challenges with finances, but practicing open and honest communication regarding money can help minimize some of the financial stressors ahead.

When you bring a child into the world, your financial sphere will be affected. Having and raising a child is generally a fairly expensive endeavor. From increased food and clothing costs to diapers, car seats, and strollers, there can be many additional expenses in the first year alone. As your child grows, many of the added costs will grow with them. It's important to plan ahead as much as possible to lower your financial stress.

Finances Conversations

Conversation 11

How do you currently handle money between the two of you? Do you have a budget? Are both of you working? Do you currently contribute to a joint fund for your daily living needs (food, housing, utilities, etc.)? Do you have separate accounts? Do you have healthcare and retirement benefits with your jobs?

Action Item

Complete a financial assessment together on the attached grid. If you do not have a budget, there are tools online to help you create one.

I (birth mother) am employed full-time.
I am employed part-time.
I am not employed.
My partner is employed full-time.
My partner is employed part-time.
My partner is not employed.
We have only a joint account for our family expenses.
We have separate accounts for our personal or family expenses.
We have both a joint account and separate accounts.
I have health insurance for our family.
My partner has health insurance for our family.
I have disability insurance.
My partner has disability insurance.
I have life insurance for my partner.
My partner has life insurance for me.
I have money in a retirement account.
My partner has money in a retirement account.
Other financial considerations:

Conversation 12

What is your plan around work when your baby arrives? How much time will one or both of you take off from work? Will the birth mother return to work, and if so, full-time or part-time? Will either partner stay home? If so, will this put more pressure on the primary earner to work longer hours or find a different job? Will your benefits be affected? Will you have family watching your child, or will you be paying for child care?

Action Item

Complete the following grid together. Discuss your answers.

Birth Mother:
I plan to take off this much time after our baby arrives:
I plan to return to my current employment at this time:
I plan to not return to my current employment or am not currently employed.
Based on the above, my benefits will be affected in these ways:
My partner plans to take off this much time after our baby arrives:
My partner is not currently employed or is unable to take any time off of work.
Based on the above, my partner's benefits will be affected in these ways:
When I return to work, we plan to have our child in daycare. Number of hours/days per week:
When I return to work, we plan to have family watch our child. Number of hours/days per week:
When I return to work, we plan to have someone we hire watch our child. Number of hours/days per week:

Conversation 13

Many estimates of raising a child in a middle-class family in the United States run about $14,000 per year (in 2020). What plans do you have in place to cover increased expenses after your child is born? (Diapers, increased insurance costs, child care, etc.)

Action Item

Estimate the costs of the following items together by looking up average costs online. In what ways might you be able to lower these costs if you wish, such as gathering some items from friends or family who no longer need them, asking for some items at a baby shower, or discussing which items are negotiable?

Cost estimations during your baby's first year
Child care: $ per month
Diapers: $ per month
Formula/Baby food: $ per month
Baby clothes: $ per month
Car seat: $
Stroller: $
Sleeping space (crib/co-sleeper): $
Baby's room: $
Increased health care insurance costs: $ per month
Other: $

Conversation 14

No one really wants to imagine the unthinkable. But, have you and your partner set up wills and designated guardians for your baby in the event of your unexpected deaths?

Action Item

There are free tools online to create a last will and testament. Alternatively, call a trusted lawyer and create a comprehensive will to assure your wishes are followed, and your child is protected in the event of a parent's untimely death.

Roles

In a partnership, people tend to gravitate toward particular roles. Some people may enjoy making dinner, folding the laundry, paying the bills, or shoveling snow, while their partners are more than happy not to do those things. Every partnership will have a process for determining what is most helpful or functional in the relationship related to roles, whether it is spoken about or not.

When there is a need for significant restructuring within a family system, such as in the case of having a child, tensions often arise because the roles frequently need to shift. For example, if the birth mother has traditionally been the money manager in the partnership but is now struggling to stay awake postpartum, they may need some support from their partner in managing the money. It can be helpful to understand roles may completely shift in the time following birth. It takes many weeks, at the very least, for a birth mother to heal properly and regain energy for anything other than the baby. This is a good time to have extra help available and keep your expectations of each other around your pre-baby roles low.

Good communication is essential, including verbal appreciation for the things each partner does currently and in their future relationship with the baby. It can be beneficial to clearly define your present roles and how these may shift in the short- and long-term after your baby's arrival. Being transparent about your needs will help you anticipate changes and find ways to build more flexibility into your family system.

Roles Conversations

Conversation 15

What do your roles look like presently in your relationship? How do you split up household chores? Who pays the bills? Does your current arrangement feel like it works well for you?

Action Item

Complete the following grid together. Discuss your answers.

Current Roles	Partner A	Both	Partner B
Grocery shopping			
Laundry			
Cooking meals			
Cleaning home			
Paying bills			
Yard work			
Home maintenance			
Car maintenance			
Pet care			
Other -			
Other -			
Other -			
This arrangement feels good to me.			

I (partner A) would like this arrangement to shift in this/ these way(s):

I (partner B) would like this arrangement to shift in this/ these way(s):

Conversation 16

How do you imagine your roles may change after your baby arrives? Will one or both of you stay home with your baby for a certain amount of time? Are there unspoken expectations about what the role shifts will be? For example, if one person stays home with the baby, are they doing all the household chores? What kind of arrangements can you set up *now* to prepare for role changes, considering the different factors that will affect your family? For example: if the birth mother will return to work, if you have help and for how long, if you and your baby are not sleeping, etc. Also, consider how these responsibilities might evolve as your baby gets older and how you might adjust the division of these chores and responsibilities.

Action Item

Complete the following grid together. Discuss how you might best support each other with role shifts.

Roles Postpartum	Partner A	Both	Partner B
I imagine our roles will stay the same as during pregnancy.			
I imagine our roles will shift in these ways:			
Grocery shopping			
Laundry			
Cooking meals			
Cleaning home			
Paying bills			
Yard work			
Other -			
Other -			
Other -			
Additional Roles:			
Daily watching of Baby			
Nighttime feeding/ soothing of Baby			
Diaper-changing			
Bathing Baby			
Other -			
I imagine our roles will shift for this amount of time:			
During the above time, I imagine we will have extra support.			

I imagine these people will help support us:

Arrangements we can set up *now* to prepare for role changes:

How these responsibilities might evolve as our baby gets older:

Self-Care

Self-care is about taking care of your physical, mental, and emotional well-being. Good self-care is critical in order to be the best version of yourself. Consider the times in your life where you may not have taken the best care of your body—skimping on sleep, not paying enough attention to the foods you eat, or not moving your body enough. Consider the times in your life when you may have neglected yourself mentally or emotionally—working too hard, not making time to be socially engaged, or not having fun. It is nearly impossible to consistently neglect any of these things without eventually becoming sick or unhappy.

When a child arrives, free time is at a premium. Some people find their exercise, nutrition, and sleep needs either increase or decrease after having a baby.

Some people find some of their friends fade into the background, while new friendships with others who have young children may develop. Some individuals find they don't have the energy for their usual hobbies or date nights with their partner.

Determining your current self-care needs and which ones are non-negotiable can help you plan for the time after your baby arrives. Recognizing how you replenish yourselves will allow you and your partner to best support one another.

Self-Care Conversations

Conversation 17

What do you currently do to take care of yourself physically? How much exercise or other physical movement do you get each day or week? What kinds of exercise or movement? How do you imagine this might change after your baby arrives?

Action Item

Complete the following grid together. Discuss how you might best support each other to get your exercise or other movement needs met.

Partner A					
How many minutes per day I currently exercise/move:					
Types of exercise/movement:					

Partner B					
How many minutes per day I currently exercise/move:					
Types of exercise/movement:					

Partner A	1 month	3 months	6 months	9 months	12 months
How many minutes per day I hope to exercise/move when our baby is:					
Types of exercise/ movement:					

Partner B	1 month	3 months	6 months	9 months	12 months
How many minutes per day I hope to exercise/move when our baby is:					
Types of exercise/ movement:					

Conversation 18

How do you feel about the health of your dietary habits? Does what you eat give you energy and stamina? Are there any things about your diet you would like to change to improve your health? How do you imagine your nutritional needs and habits might change after your baby arrives?

Action Item

Complete the following grid together. Discuss how you might best support each other to get your nutritional needs met.

What I eat gives me energy and stamina.					
Partner A	never	seldom	sometimes	frequently	always
Partner B	never	seldom	sometimes	frequently	always

Ways I might like to improve my eating habits:
Partner A
Partner B

How my nutritional needs and habits might change after our baby is born:

Partner A at:	1 month	3 months	6 months	9 months	12 months
I imagine I will be very concerned about what I eat.					
I imagine I will not be very concerned about what I eat.					
I imagine I will eat more than I usually do.					
I imagine I will eat less than I usually do.					

	1 month	3 months	6 months	9 months	12 months
I imagine I will eat about the same amount I usually do.					

How my nutritional needs and habits might change after our baby is born:

Partner B at:	1 month	3 months	6 months	9 months	12 months
I imagine I will be very concerned about what I eat.					
I imagine I will not be very concerned about what I eat.					
I imagine I will eat more than I usually do.					
I imagine I will eat less than I usually do.					
I imagine I will eat about the same amount as I usually do.					

Conversation 19

How much sleep do you currently get per night? Do you wake up feeling refreshed? Do you have an energy slump during the day? If so, how do you pick your energy back up? How do you imagine your sleep might be affected after your baby is born?

Action Item

Complete the following grid together. Discuss how you might best support each other to get your sleep needs met.

Average number of hours I sleep per night:			
Partner A		hours	
Partner B		hours	
This feels like enough sleep for me.			
Partner A	Yes	Usually	No
Partner B	Yes	Usually	No
Partner A I have an energy slump during the day.	Yes	Usually	No
Approximate time of energy slump:			
How I pick myself back up:			
Partner B I have an energy slump during the day.	Yes	Usually	No
Approximate time of energy slump:			
How I pick myself back up:			
How I imagine my sleep might be affected after our baby is born:			
Partner A			
Partner B			

Conversation 20

Who are your close friends? How much time do you spend with your friends? Does each partner have their own friends as well as mutual friends? How do you imagine your friend connections might change or other friendships might develop during pregnancy and after your baby arrives?

Action Item

Complete the following grid together. Discuss how you might best support each other to get your social needs met.

Who my closest individual friends are:					
Partner A					
Partner B					
How often I see my friends currently:					
Partner A					
Partner B					
This feels like enough time.					
Partner A	never	seldom	sometimes	frequently	always
Partner B	never	seldom	sometimes	frequently	always
Who our closest mutual friends are:					
How often we see our mutual friends currently:					
This feels like enough time.					
Partner A	never	seldom	sometimes	frequently	always
Partner B	never	seldom	sometimes	frequently	always
Other people I like to spend time with:					
Partner A					
Partner B					
Ways in which friendships may change or new friendships may develop during pregnancy and after having a baby:					
Partner A					
Partner B					

Conversation 21

How often do you engage in a hobby? How important
are your hobbies for you? How do you imagine time
for hobbies might change after your baby arrives?

Action Item

Complete the following grid together. Discuss how you might best support each other to get your needs for maintaining your hobbies met.

Partner A		
Favorite hobbies	Amount of time I spend engaging in this hobby per week.	How much I hope to engage in this hobby per week after our baby arrives.
Partner B		
Favorite hobbies	Amount of time I spend engaging in this hobby per week.	How much I hope to engage in this hobby per week after our baby arrives.

Conversation 22

How do you currently negotiate with your partner around both of your self-care needs? For example, how do you plan time into your schedules for each of you to get exercise or go out with friends? How do you balance this with your needs for couple-time, such as a date night or time you plan to spend together at home? How do you imagine this schedule might change after your baby arrives?

Action Item (part 1)

Complete the following grid together. Discuss how you might best support each other to get your self-care needs met.

I discuss my self-care needs with my partner.					
Partner A	never	seldom	sometimes	frequently	always
Partner B	never	seldom	sometimes	frequently	always
I have enough time to take care of my self-care needs.					
Partner A	never	seldom	sometimes	frequently	always
Partner B	never	seldom	sometimes	frequently	always
Partner A					
Some of my self-care needs are neglected.	never	seldom	sometimes	frequently	always
These are the self-care needs I feel are neglected:					
Partner B					
Some of my self-care needs are neglected.	never	seldom	sometimes	frequently	always
These are the self-care needs I feel are neglected:					

Action Item (part 2)

Make individual lists of the top five to ten self-care activities that are most important for your overall health and well-being. Share these lists and discuss with your partner why they are important. Decide which needs on your self-care list are the most essential to try to meet after your baby is born, when free time is more limited. Share how you plan to try to stay connected through dates or activities at home together.

Partner A	**Partner B**
1. _____	1. _____
2. _____	2. _____
3. _____	3. _____
4. _____	4. _____
5. _____	5. _____
6. _____	6. _____
7. _____	7. _____
8. _____	8. _____
9. _____	9. _____
10. _____	10. _____

Preparing for Parenthood

Values

Values are the beliefs you hold and the way these beliefs affect how you see and act in the world. Understanding the values you grew up with and how they may have changed over time is essential in deciding how you will raise your own children. Knowing what is most important to you and your partner and utilizing this information to facilitate decision-making is a significant step toward creating the family experience you desire.

General Values Conversations

Conversation 23

What were the most important values you were each raised with that may impact your family life? How do your values complement each other? How might they conflict? Use the values list below as a starting point to jump off from.

eat dinner together	apologize after an argument	spend time outdoors
have patience	belief in religion/ spirituality	honesty is the best policy
trust should be earned	hard work brings good results	achieve academically
be frugal with money	family comes first	healthy work-life balance
take care of the earth	take responsibility for your actions	be dependable
take risks	be of service to others	express gratitude
be tolerant of others	humor is the best medicine	play
don't give up	treat others as you would like to be treated	

Action Item

Write down what values you grew up with. Indicate the values you still hold as important in your adult life by placing a star next to them.

Partner A	**Partner B**
1. _____	1. _____
2. _____	2. _____
3. _____	3. _____
4. _____	4. _____
5. _____	5. _____
6. _____	6. _____
7. _____	7. _____
8. _____	8. _____
9. _____	9. _____
10. _____	10. _____

Conversation 24

What are the most important values you hope to raise your child with? Does your partner share these same values? If not, what is your plan for working through these differences?

Action Item

Write down the values you hope to raise your child with and number them in order of importance. Share your list with your partner. If there are discrepancies between your lists, is there a similar underlying value where you can find a place to compromise? For example, if you love hiking and your partner loves lounging on a beach, can you compromise in terms of the similar underlying value of hoping to enjoy the outdoors as a family? Use the values list from Conversation 23 as a starting point, if needed.

Partner A	**Partner B**
1.	1.
2.	2.
3.	3.
4.	4.
5.	5.
6.	6.
7.	7.
8.	8.
9.	9.
10.	10.

Religion & Spirituality

Conversation 25

What role did religion or spirituality play for you growing up? What role does religion or spirituality play for you currently?

Action Item

Discuss your religious or spiritual beliefs with your partner. Share all of the elements of your religion or spirituality you felt were helpful to you when growing up. Were there any unhelpful pieces? If so, what were they, and why weren't they helpful? Discuss with your partner how you incorporate religion or spirituality into your life currently together. If you come from different spiritual backgrounds, clarify with your partner how you navigate these differences as a couple.

Conversation 26

What role might religion or spirituality play in your life as a family? What beliefs or practices would you like to instill in your child? How do you imagine that might look practically for your family?

Action Item

Design a plan with your partner around how you imagine religion or spirituality will look in a practical sense in your family. For example, will you attend a particular house of worship, celebrate certain holidays, mark certain rites of passage, and/or create ceremonies of your own?

Education

Conversation 27

What are your hopes for your child around preschool education? What kind of preschool education are you interested in for your child?

Action Item

Begin researching the various preschool choices in your area or asking friends with preschool-aged children about their experiences at different preschools.

Conversation 28

Do you and your partner have the same ideas about what type of grade school education you would like your child to receive—public school, private school, homeschool, etc.?

Action Item

Clarify with your partner what your hopes and plans are for your child's grade-school education. This may involve looking at the available schools where you live (elementary, middle, and high schools) and determining what type of school would make a good fit based on your hopes for your child.

Health Care

Conversation 29

What are your beliefs around health care for your child? Do you plan to follow Western medicine guidelines, alternative medicine guidelines, or a combination of the two? Why have you made this decision?

Action Item

Clarify with your partner your beliefs around health care for your child and why you have made this decision.

Conversation 30

Do you have health insurance? If so, what does it cover? What will it cover for your child, and what might be some out-of-pocket expenses you will have?

Action Item

Research what expenses will be covered for your child on your current plan, from pregnancy through childbirth and onward. What will your increased expenses look like?

Conversation 31

Vaccination has been a controversial topic over the past years in some regions of the country and world. How do each of you feel about vaccinating your child? Is it important for you to follow the recommended Western medicine child immunization schedule beginning with vaccinations given at birth? Are there any vaccines you have questions about? Are you considering a delayed or alternative vaccination schedule? If so, what are your reasons for your choices? What are the current applicable laws in your state regarding immunization, in terms of how this might affect child care (and later, school) eligibility? How might your choices affect your ability to travel, if needed or desired?

Action Item

Check with your healthcare provider or other trusted resources for information regarding vaccinations and the recommended Western medicine immunization schedule. Working with your partner, create a plan around vaccinating that feels comfortable for both of you.

Conversation 32

If you have a boy, what are your feelings around circumcision? What beliefs guide these feelings for each of you?

Action Item

Check with your healthcare provider or other trusted resources for information regarding circumcision. Come up with a plan you both feel comfortable with regarding this decision.

Discipline

Discipline is a way of teaching. It is different than punishment. Punishment focuses on trying to control a child's behavior through fear or intimidation. Children learn what behavior is *bad* and try to avoid being caught doing that behavior only because they don't want the punishment. Discipline, on the other hand, helps teach children natural consequences and how their actions affect themselves and others. This opens up communication between the parent and child, helps to develop empathy and understanding of a wider social code of behavior, and encourages the child to learn from and take responsibility for their actions. Both partners need to be on the same page around discipline, so parenting can occur as a team.

Discipline Conversations

Conversation 33

How did your parents or caregivers discipline you? What aspects of their discipline did you appreciate or not appreciate?

Action Item

Clarify with your partner which methods of discipline your parents or caregivers used that worked for you, and which, if any, felt more like punishment than discipline. Discuss how you each feel about your own parents' discipline and how it affected you.

Conversation 34

What are your beliefs around discipline with your child? Would you incorporate different disciplinary measures than those you grew up with?

Action Item

Research different strategies for using discipline with your child to see which one(s) you both feel most aligned with.

Your History

O ur early experiences and emotions in life, even those we don't clearly remember, can have a profound impact on our present life. The ages from zero to three especially create a unique foundation for how we see and experience the world. Greater awareness and integration of your own history can allow for deeper empathy for your child and their experiences. This awareness and integration can also help you recognize and alter your reactions to your child's behaviors.

It is worth the effort to understand your history and gain support for any unhealed emotional wounds that may be affecting your present life. Learning to respond rather than react under stress in parenting can be an ongoing practice. But parenting from a place of integrated health and presence is one of the greatest gifts you can offer your child.

For this section, it may be useful to talk with someone from your family of origin, if possible. Also, some of the following questions may spark strong emotions for some readers. Please be sure to seek support from your partner, close friends, a therapist, or another support person, if needed.

Your History Conversations

Conversation 35

What do you know about your birth mother's experience of being pregnant with you and your parents' relationship with each other at that time? What do you know about your birth mother's experience of giving birth to you?

Action Item

If you have access to your birth mother, invite the sharing of what it was like to be pregnant with and give birth to you. Write down as much information about this time as you can. Look for the emotional content of what is shared. For example, was your birth mother relaxed and happy during pregnancy? Was there any excessive stress during your birth? If you have access to your biological father, invite the same sharing of experiences. If you have access to neither, you may gain some information from your birth and medical records, siblings, extended family members, or family friends.

Conversation 36

What do you know about your experiences during your first three years of life? With whom did you spend most of your time? What are your positive memories of those times? What were some of the challenges you faced? For example, what do you know about your caregivers and your experiences with eating, sleeping, and reaching developmental milestones?

Action Item

If you have access to your caregivers from when you were young, ask them to share stories, old photographs, or any other information to help you understand your early years.

Conversation 37

What do you recall about your later childhood, adolescence, and early adulthood years? What are your positive memories of those times? What were some of the challenges you faced? For example, was school enjoyable? How did you spend your free time? Who were your closest friends? What are your memories of being at home with your caregivers and siblings? What was your life like once you left home?

Action Item

If you have access to your caregivers who were present during your later childhood and adolescent years, ask them to share stories, old photographs, or any other information to help in your understanding. If you have siblings or extended family members, ask them for stories. Delve into your memories of these times, including your early adult years—school, friends, family experiences—and think about which memories stand out to you.

Pregnancy

Couples may experience pregnancy in many different ways. You may both feel excited, nervous, downright scared, ecstatic, emotional, physically ill, better than you've ever felt, or sometimes a combination of any of these things in the span of a given day. You may think there is a lot to get ready for before your baby arrives, or you may feel relaxed about it all. Your body, or your partner's body, will change substantially in a short time as it grows a little human being.

Pregnancy Conversations

Conversation 38

From whom will you seek prenatal care and advice (doctor, midwife, etc.)? From what sources will you get information about all other things related to pregnancy (friends, books, blogs, podcasts, videos, etc.)?

Action Item

Decide what kind of prenatal care you would like to receive and whom you might want to provide that care. Set up an initial appointment, and arrive with a list of questions you might have. To begin to educate yourself about pregnancy, take a trip to a local library or bookstore to browse the available pregnancy books. Reach out to friends who have had babies, or find a blog or podcast you enjoy.

Conversation 39

What prenatal testing are you interested in obtaining? For example, are you interested in receiving multiple blood tests, ultrasounds, genetic testing, amniocentesis, etc.? Are there any prenatal tests you have concerns about or are opposed to? If you were to receive unexpected test results regarding your health or the health of your baby, and if difficult decisions needed to be made, are you and your partner aligned about how you would make these decisions together and with your healthcare provider?

Action Item

Research what prenatal testing is available. What does your healthcare provider recommend? Discuss any concerns with your partner and what your plan would be moving forward if you received unexpected test results.

Conversation 40

What kind of support network can you begin building for yourselves now to help sustain you throughout pregnancy, birth, and into the postpartum period? For example, you may be interested in joining a prenatal exercise class where you may meet others who would like to connect for postpartum exercise.

Action Item

Look into groups in your area where you could expand your support network. Consider aiming to connect with at least one person or couple with whom you could continue to communicate after your children are born.

Conversation 41

Though most people don't like to think about it, sometimes complications occur during pregnancy. For example, there may be challenges with maintaining a pregnancy, or the baby may begin the birthing process much sooner than anticipated. How emotionally ready do you both feel to navigate any challenges?

Action Item

Think about whom you each would turn to (besides your partner) if you received upsetting news during your pregnancy. Emotional support during and after pregnancy is critical. Sometimes, if both you and your partner have experienced the same challenge, you may benefit from seeking outside emotional support from extended family, friends, a therapist, or other support people.

Conversation 42

Many individuals suffer from prenatal and postpartum mood disorders. Anxiety and depression can be serious mental health challenges during pregnancy and throughout the first year of your baby's life, and can also occur in partners. Do you and your partner know the symptoms to look for in prenatal and postpartum mood disorders? Who will you contact for support if you see any of the common symptoms found in these challenges?

Action Item

Become familiar with the symptoms of prenatal and postpartum mood disorders. Ask your health care provider for the contact information of mental health care providers they would recommend. Keep this information on hand in the event it is needed. A useful resource is Postpartum Support International, an organization that helps people dealing with mood disorders that happen during pregnancy and throughout the first year of your baby's life: www.postpartum.net.

Birth

Birth is a unique experience for each birth mother, partner, and baby. Many factors play into how a baby makes their way into the world, some of which you will likely have some control over, and others which you may not. It can be helpful to begin imagining the kind of birth you hope to have, while also keeping in mind your birth may be slightly-to-very different than you imagine.

Birth Conversations

Conversation 43

Where do you hope and plan to give birth to your baby (hospital, birth center, home)? From whom will you seek support during the birth (your partner, medical staff, a family member or friend, a doula, etc.)? Of these support people, who would you like to have in the room with you during your birth?

Action Item

Together, come up with a clear plan about where you hope to give birth and why you have chosen that particular place. Decide who you want to support your family during the birth experience, and what kind of specific support you'd like from them.

Conversation 44

How will you prepare for the birth? Does your healthcare provider offer birth classes? Do specific kinds of classes interest you that may be offered outside your healthcare provider's office?

Action Item

Research what birth classes are offered by your healthcare provider, as well as any other classes in your community. Research when birth mothers and their partners generally take these classes during their pregnancy, and create a plan for scheduling the classes.

Conversation 45

How do you hope the birth will go? How do you
hope to handle the experience if the birth does not
go as anticipated? If, for whatever reason, your birth
goes differently than you had expected, and you find
yourself upset, whom can you turn to for support?

Action Item

Write down your hopes for your birth in detail. Research and keep a list of people you can turn to for support if needed.

Early Parenthood

Postpartum

The time following the birth of your first baby can be many things—blissful, unsettling, relaxed, nerve-wracking, exhausting, etc. But one thing is certain—we are not designed to transition to parenthood in isolation. There are tremendous benefits to receiving extensive support during the early postpartum time. In preparing for this phase, it is important to rally your troops, and these troops may be people you haven't even met yet. Often new parents find they need the support of others going through a similar transition to parenthood—people who really get what it is like for them currently. This is where finding others who are about to become parents, or who have recently become parents, can be immensely valuable. Preparing for postpartum support ahead of time will likely allow you to avoid a great deal of discomfort during this time when you may feel too overwhelmed to reach out for help.

Postpartum Conversations

Conversation 46

What support network will be available to you post-birth? Do you have family nearby, or will they be visiting? What about friends? Are there people available to make food or meet other needs for your family during the first few weeks postpartum?

Action Item

Create a list of family and friends who are suited to help your family with different needs, such as making food, doing laundry, caring for the baby so you can sleep, staying with the birth mother and baby during post-birth healing, etc. Consider asking a family member or friend to organize extended support for you through one of the many online scheduling systems.

Conversation 47

If the birth mother was working before birth and plans to return to work afterward, how many weeks/ months will be taken off for leave? How will your support system change during and after that time? Will your partner have work leave and stay home?

Action Item

Complete the following grid showing the number of weeks/months the birth mother and partner will have off from work and the type of support you will arrange for during that time.

Number of weeks/months we will have off from work.	# of weeks	# of months
Partner A		
Partner B		
Support we will have, and from whom.	Names	
Emotional support:		
Making food for us:		
Shopping for us:		
Daily help with our baby:		
Laundry or light house cleaning:		
Other support:		

Conversation 48

What groups can you join now, or what individuals can you connect with to build the support you will need as new parents? For example, are there prenatal and birth classes you can join to meet others who are about to have babies? Are there new parents' groups you can learn about in your area?

Action Item

Research what groups are available in your area and online. Find a new parents' group, a prenatal class, a birth class, or other support groups that may appeal to you. Begin creating future support by connecting with others who are also becoming parents.

Sleep

Newborn babies tend to sleep a great deal. However, *when* they sleep may not necessarily coincide with when you want to sleep. In utero, babies experience relative darkness most of the time. Their eyes are closed. They sleep and eat when they need to.

Once babies are born, this doesn't shift right away. Babies will still sleep when they need to. They will want to eat when they are hungry. Because they have tiny bellies, they need to eat frequently, including during the middle of the night. Additionally, they are used to being *held* (in the birth mother's uterus) all of the time.

Being out in the world is a huge change, and it takes a while for most babies to adjust. But it also takes time for parents to adjust. Most new parents have times when they are not sleeping well because the baby is frequently waking or has trouble getting to sleep.

Sleep is critical to our well-being throughout life. While many researchers believe different sleep patterns are largely wired into our systems, there are often ways to help promote good sleep habits for parents and babies. Assuming sleep will be a challenge and discussing ways to address these challenges before everyone is sleep-deprived will help you navigate this important issue.

Sleep Conversations

Conversation 49

Where would you like your baby to sleep? For example, will the baby sleep in a co-sleeper or bassinet next to the parents' bed, in a crib in their own room, etc.? This may look different over time as your baby grows older.

Action Item

Research different sleeping options, and find a couple of options you feel comfortable with. Build flexibility into your decisions. Many parents imagine their baby will sleep one way but find they need to make different arrangements if this is not working for their family.

Conversation 50

What are your plans for support if your baby isn't sleeping very much and you probably aren't either?

Action Item

Research infant sleep specialists in your area (or online), or find a couple of books detailing sleep support, should you find you need these. Check with your support network (friends who have infants, etc.) to find out what challenges they might have had and what has worked for them.

Conversation 51

We are not at our best when sleep-deprived. We may feel irritable, spacey, or emotional. We may have difficulty being patient with and supportive of our partner. How will you take care of yourself and each other as a couple if you're both sleep-deprived?

Action Item

Come up with a code word or phrase you can use as a couple to let your partner know you are suffering from a lack of sleep and need support, such as, "I'm cooked," or, "I need a nap." Expect to need to take a nap sometimes, or to give up plans, to make sure each partner can catch up on some lost sleep.

Feeding and Diapering

Feeding your baby can take many different forms—from breastfeeding, to pumping for bottles, to formula, and any combination of these. Nevertheless, newborn babies need milk, and their little bellies need it often. Having a flexible plan in place about your feeding choices and needs can help you prepare as a couple. Most parents also choose to diaper their babies, and there are many decisions around this as well.

Feeding & Diapering Conversations

Conversation 52

Do you hope or plan to breastfeed? If so, for how long do you hope this will happen? What is your plan if there are challenges with breastfeeding? Do you hope to bottle-feed or try a combination of breastfeeding and bottle-feeding? Various factors could influence this choice, such as if the birth mother is returning to work, if the partner would like to be involved with feeding the baby, etc. How can you prepare for bottle-feeding now?

Action Item

If you hope or plan to breastfeed, begin doing some research about the topic. For some people, breastfeeding is an easy adjustment, but for others, it isn't. Breastfeeding may not be possible for some. Learn about breastfeeding before your baby arrives to give you a better understanding of what is involved. Also, consider the length of time you wish to breastfeed, and be sure you and your partner are on the same page. This will look different given your unique family situation—for example, if/when the birth mother returns to work, if you are planning to have another baby within a certain time frame, etc. It can be beneficial to create a list of individuals or organizations to contact before you have your baby, should you encounter any later breastfeeding challenges. Have the names of a couple of recommended lactation consultants in your area, and research breastfeeding support organizations in your area (and internationally online), such as La Leche League: www.llli.org. Also, consider what you might need to have on hand if you choose to bottle-feed. Research breast pumps and formula you feel comfortable with. Decide what kind of bottles you would like to use (glass, plastic, different nipple choices), and purchase them ahead of time.

Conversation 53

What are your plans around diapering? Are you planning to use disposable or cloth diapers, or a combination? Do you hope to use a diaper service in your area? Are both partners comfortable changing and perhaps washing diapers? What about night diaper changes?

Action Item

Research different diapering options by talking with friends, researching online, and discussing your diapering hopes and expectations of each other.

Gratitude & Visioning

When we had our first baby, we felt like the luckiest humans on the entire planet. We loved holding our little daughter, drinking in her new-baby smell, kissing her tiny feet, and seeing her beautiful eyes open up to take us in. This feeling multiplied after we had our second daughter; the love and awe expanded and enveloped our family. Our children have changed and continue to change our lives in wondrous, positive ways, and we are deeply grateful.

I grew exponentially as an individual when I became a parent. I learned to slow down, developed more patience, expanded my ability to manage challenging things when I thought I had reached my limit, and experienced daily how much larger my heart could feel with my family. We also grew tremendously as a couple when we became parents. We learned how to negotiate more effectively, how to be gentler with each other when we were under stress, and how to work well together as a unified team. Parenting hasn't always been easy, but it has always been powerful.

There is no doubt that for most people, parenthood is an incredible gift. It is a privilege to be able to birth a new life and an honor to raise a human being into adulthood. It is also a gift to experience *raising yourself* as a parent, growing right alongside your child. However, there may be times when your ability to feel this privilege is challenged. We all have times as parents or parents-to-be where circumstances or events feel difficult. Hopefully, throughout completing this book, you've found ways to both normalize and help lessen some of those challenges as you embark on this journey.

As you continue your parenting voyage, I invite you to keep the big picture in mind. When a new baby arrives, both partners will likely find they need to step up to meet many challenges in ways that may stretch them. However, like all relationships, parenting is a journey requiring an ongoing learning process. There will always be opportunities to grow, change, and connect. There is no one right way to parent. You're going to hear a great deal of advice about parenting with many different viewpoints, but ultimately, you'll need to discover what works for you and your family.

You'll make mistakes—probably lots of them. Remember, you don't need to be a perfect parent. If you do a solid job the majority of the time, your children will be okay. Children are quite resilient and forgiving. An apology and the ability to repair will go a long way toward healing mistakes and will also model for your children that adults are human beings who sometimes make errors. This will allow your child to feel safe enough to take risks and make mistakes because they know you will be there to support and forgive them.

I encourage you to focus on your strengths. Be gentle with your shortcomings as you cross the threshold into parenthood. Keep finding and turning toward the positives. Cherish those things that bring joy to you about parenthood. Emphasize what you can do instead of what you feel unable to do. Focus on your child's laughter and hugs instead of their tantrums, and bask in the little everyday pleasures that come with parenting. Celebrate every precious day you have with your child, no matter what their age.

Gratitude & Visioning Conversations

Conversation 54

What are you most grateful for right now in your own life, and in your lives together? How do you share your gratitude as a couple? What do you love and appreciate most about your partner? What qualities do you believe you'll appreciate most about them as a parent?

Action Item

If you don't already have a ritual for sharing appreciations or gratitude, create one. For example, share one thing you appreciate or are grateful for at the end of the day when you sit down for dinner. Find a ritual that feels authentic and positive for you as a family. Share your appreciation often with each other, and with your child when they arrive.

Conversation 55

I want to leave you with one final conversation, one that will hopefully become a platform for jumping into the many other discussions you will have together as parents. What are your hopes and dreams for your family? Envision your family and family life becoming what you imagined it would become. What activities do you share? How do you relate to one another? What makes your family *your* family? Is yours a family who enjoys a lot of laughter? Do you pursue outdoor adventures? Do you read books or play music together? Do you travel? Do you have heady discussions at the dinner table? Try to be as specific as possible about what your vision for your family looks like. Then, share your vision with your partner. Bring your two separate visions together to create a shared vision for your family.

Action Item

Imagine your shared vision for your family is happening right now in the present. What does it look and feel like? Use all of your senses to bring your vision to life. Write down your shared vision together as a couple, or create a drawing or collage that shows your biggest hopes for your family. Revisit your vision often to be sure you are helping keep it alive, and update it as needed.

Made in United States
North Haven, CT
21 July 2022

21609642R00124